This notebook belongs to:

Made in the USA
Monee, IL
03 October 2021

79286602R00073